DARING DINOSAUR

THIS EDITION
Produced for DK by WonderLab Group LLC
Jennifer Emmett, Erica Green, Kate Hale, **Founders**

Editor Maya Myers; **Photography Editor** Nicole DiMella; **Managing Editor** Rachel Houghton;
Designers Project Design Company; **Researcher** Michelle Harris; **Copy Editor** Lori Merritt;
Indexer Connie Binder; **Proofreader** Susan K. Hom;
Series Reading Specialist Dr. Jennifer Albro; **Paleontology Expert** Akiko Shinya

First American Edition, 2025
Published in the United States by DK Publishing, a division of Penguin Random House LLC
1745 Broadway, 20th Floor, New York, NY 10019

Design copyright © Dorling Kindersley Limited 2025
Text and Illustration copyright © WonderLab Group LLC 2025
24 25 26 27 10 9 8 7 6 5 4 3 2 1
001–345520–April/2025

All rights reserved.
Without limiting the rights under the copyright reserved above, no part of this publication may be reproduced, stored in or introduced into a retrieval system, or transmitted, in any form, or by any means (electronic, mechanical, photocopying, recording, or otherwise), without the prior written permission of the copyright owner.
Published in Great Britain by Dorling Kindersley Limited

A catalog record for this book is available from the Library of Congress.
HC ISBN: 978-0-5939-6600-6
PB ISBN: 978-0-5939-6599-3

DK books are available at special discounts when purchased in bulk for sales promotions, premiums, fund-raising, or educational use. For details, contact:
DK Publishing Special Markets, 1745 Broadway, 20th Floor, New York, NY 10019
SpecialSales@dk.com

Printed and bound in China
Super Readers Lexile® levels 500L to 610L
Lexile® is the registered trademark of MetaMetrics, Inc. Copyright © 2024 MetaMetrics, Inc. All rights reserved.

The publisher would like to thank the following for their kind permission to reproduce their images:
a=above; c=center; b=below; l=left; r=right; t=top; b/g=background

123RF.com: Linda Bucklin 19cr, Leonello Calvetti 11tr, 25br, Mark Turner 18t; **Alamy Stock Photo:** Ton Koene 17br, MShieldsPhotos 15cra, Ghislaine BRAS / Onlyfrance.fr 9br, Science Photo Library / Roger Harris 26-27, Universal Images Group North America LLC / DeAgostini 11cl; **Dorling Kindersley:** Jon Hughes 10crb; **Dreamstime.com:** Alhovik 26cr, B0961810824 12tr, Blue Ring Education Pte Ltd 17cla, Leonello Calvetti 23c, Dewins 12bc, Roman Egorov 7cb, Daniel Eskridge 3, 16, 20b, 28bl, Corey A Ford 29br, Iadamson 26cra, Ratchanikon Klahan 12tl, Ladadikart 28c, Lewisroland 13, Irina Miroshnichenko 5bl, Mr1805 1, 3-4, 11crb, Olgakotsareva 12bl (br), Aaron Rutten 6-7, Yevheniia Ryzhova 10-11, Sofia Santos / Chastity 30b, Techa Tungateja 8-9, 28-29, Mark Turner 9cra, 10bl, 25tr, Zabiamdeve 18cl, 19crb; **Getty Images:** Angela Weiss / AFP 29tr; **Getty Images / iStock:** Zhanna Barada 17cla (dinosaur), Fendy Hermawan 26br, Evgeniya_Mokeeva 10cr, 11bc, 13cb, 23tl, 29ca, 30crb; © **Field Museum:** 24br; **Science Photo Library:** Carlton Publishing Group 28cr, Philippe Plailly 9cb; **Shutterstock.com:** Innakote 21, Dotted Yeti 14-15, YuRi Photolife 29cl

Cover images: *Front:* **Dreamstime.com:** Techa Tungateja; **Shutterstock.com:** KAMONRAT bl;
Back: **Dreamstime.com:** Daniel Eskridge cl; **Shutterstock.com:** Matis75 cra

www.dk.com

Level 2

DARING DINOSAUR

Becky Baines

Contents

- **6** Can You Dig It?
- **8** Dino Timeline
- **10** We Are Family
- **12** Mega-Munchers
- **16** Speed Racers
- **20** Built for Battle

24 Deadliest Dinos
28 Ancient All-Stars
30 Glossary
31 Index
32 Quiz

Can You Dig It?

A long, long time ago, Earth looked a lot different than it does today. Giant volcanoes erupted lava all over the land.

WHOOO! Who wants to go lava-skating?

Big deserts and super-wet forests were divided by mountains taller than three skyscrapers! And one creature ruled the land: the daring dino!

Dino Timeline

Dinosaurs were large and in charge for 165 million years! Scientists call this time in Earth's history the Mesozoic Era.

Triassic Period: 252–201 million years ago
- *Eoraptor*
- *Mussaurus*
- *Compsognathus*

Jurassic Period: 201–145 million years ago
- *Brachiosaurus*
- *Stegosaurus*
- *Archaeopteryx*

The Mesozoic Era is divided into three periods: Triassic, Jurassic, and Cretaceous. When did your favorite dinosaur live?

Cretaceous Period: 145–66 million years ago
- Spinosaurus
- Triceratops
- Tyrannosaurus

Early Human Ancestors: 26 million years ago

First Modern Humans: 300,000 years ago

We Are Family

Lots of different kinds of dinos make up the dinosaur family tree! They are separated into two groups based on the way their bones fit together.

Saurischia: Lizard-Hipped

Sauropods
The biggest dinosaurs were plant-eaters. They walked on four legs.

Theropods
These famous predators were fast runners.

Ornithiscians: Bird-Hipped

Thyreophorans
This dino family is famous for its armor.

Heterodontosaurs
These small dinos had canine teeth. Scientists think they ate plants, insects, and animals!

Ornithopods
These dinos had beaks or duck-bills.

Marginocephalians
This family of dinosaurs had big skulls with ridges or horns.

Mega-Munchers

When you think slow, steady, and supersized, think sauropod! These biggest-of-all dinosaurs ate only plants. They could grow longer than two tennis courts. And they had appetites to match!

The biggest dinosaur ever found, *Argentinosaurus*, weighed as much as 18 African elephants. Elephants spend 80 percent of their day eating hundreds of pounds of leaves.

Scientists figured out that *Argentinosaurus* had to eat up to 2,000 pounds in plants each day to survive. Good thing dinosaurs had dino-sized trees to snack from!

Sauropods were gentle giants. They would never eat a fellow dino. But other dinosaurs still had to watch out! Fossilized footprints tell us that sauropods roamed in groups. Imagine getting caught in a sauropod stampede!

Speed Racers

When it came to speed, one family of dinos had the others beat by a mile. Ornithopods didn't have big teeth. They were not huge. Many of them survived because they were fast.

Just call me the Flash from the Past!

One of the fastest dinosaurs was *Gallimimus*. It looked like an ostrich. It could run in bursts at 50 miles an hour (80 km/h). That's almost as fast as cars drive on the highway!

I could beat these birdbrains when I'm dino-snoring!

Running the Numbers

Ancient dinos have been extinct for many millions of years. So, scientists have to estimate dino speed. The fastest animals in the world today have long lower leg bones. Scientists can tell if a dino was speedy by looking at fossils of its leg bones.

Another group of speedsters were the dromaeosaurids. They are often called raptors. They were a type of theropod—cousins of the famous *Tyrannosaurus rex.*

These dinos could be as small as a dog or as big as a school bus! They had sharp teeth, long claws, and bodies built for running. Speed and strength made them deadly predators.

Built for Battle

Armored dinosaurs didn't need speed on their side. Their built-in armor and weapons made sure no one made a meal of them!

Ankylosaurus is often called a living tank. It was covered in a shell of bony plates. This "armor" was almost impossible for bigger dinos to break through. *Ankylosaurus* also swung a big club on the end of its tail. Ouch! That's one tough dino!

Stegosaurus had long, hard plates sticking straight up from its back. These plates may have helped keep the dino cool in the steamy summer heat. But it also made predators think twice about attacking. That super-spiky tail would scare them off, too!

Triceratops were famous for their long horns and frilled faces. They used their big skulls to duel their enemies. One headbutt from these guys would even send *T. rex* running!

Deadliest Dinos

There was no shortage of big, deadly dinos on land. There were whale-sized sharks in the ocean. Airplane-sized *pterosaurs* swooped through the sky. The prehistoric world was full of predators!

Spinosaurus was a huge predator. It had long crocodile-like jaws. It was the length of two fire trucks from tip to tail. It could hunt by both land and sea. Its jaws were perfect for grabbing slippery fish!

Giganotosaurus was like *T. rex*'s bigger, older cousin! It lived in the early Cretaceous period, before *T. rex*. But it had the same powerful jaws and epic claws.

Velociraptor was less than two feet (0.6 m) tall. But this guy could take down a nine-foot (2.7 m) *Triceratops*. How? It could strike just the right spot with its large claw.

Pick on someone your own size!

T. rex was a powerful predator. It was fast, with long legs perfect for chasing. Its big tail helped it turn quickly. It had big teeth and wide jaws. The strength of its bite was twice as strong as an alligator's! But it also had super senses!

The undefeated champ, 2 million years in a row!

T. rex had eyeballs the size of oranges. They helped it pinpoint hidden prey. Bones in its ear suggest it probably had super hearing. And the part of its brain used for smelling was bigger than it was in most other animals. There was no hiding from this prehistoric powerhouse!

Ancient All-Stars

Scientists have discovered over 700 different species of dinosaur. Each one is different and incredible. Check out these ancient all-stars!

Toothy Titans
Nigersaurus was a mega-muncher. Its 500 teeth replaced themselves once a month.

Can you drop me off at the dentist?

Blow that Horn
Parasaurolophus had a built-in horn on its head. Scientists think the dinosaur used it like a musical instrument!

Fanciest Fossil
Stan the *T. rex* is the best well-preserved *Tyrannosaurus* fossil ever found. He's 40 feet (12.2 m) long, 13 feet (4 m) tall, and has 188 bones!

And I thought I was strange...

Tiny Diny
Aquilops is a bunny-sized dino related to *Triceratops*!

Want to go to the nail salon?

Colossal Claws
Therizinosaurus had three-foot (1 m) claws. No one would mess with them!

Glossary

Ancestors
A distant family member from a long time ago

Cretaceous period
The last period of dinosaurs, 145 to 66 million years ago

Estimate
A best guess based on experience and observation

Fossils
The preserved remains or traces of ancient animals and plants

Jurassic period
The second period of dinosaurs, 201 to 145 million years ago

Mesozoic era
The geologic time in which all dinosaurs lived, also called the Age of Reptiles. It contained three periods: Triassic, Jurassic, and Cretaceous.

Paleontologist
A scientist who studies the history of life through fossils

Predator
An animal that hunts other animals

Prehistoric
In a time before written history

Prey
An animal that is hunted by other animals

Pterosaur
An ancient flying reptile closely related to dinosaurs

Species
A distinct group of organisms with common characteristics and can reproduce

Survive
To continue to live or exist despite difficult circumstances

Triassic period
The earliest period of dinosaurs, 252 to 201 million years ago

Index

Ankylosaurus 21

Aquilops 29

Argentinosaurus
12–13

Cretaceous period 9

dromaeosaurids
18–19

fossils 14, 17, 29

Gallimimus 17

Giganotosaurus 25

Jurassic period 8, 9

Mesozoic era 9

Nigersaurus 28

ornithiscians 11

ornithopods 11, 16–17

Parasaurolophus 28

raptors 18–19

saurischia 10

sauropods 10, 12–15

Spinosaurus 9, 24

Stegosaurus 8, 22

Therizinosaurus 29

theropods 10, 18–19

timeline 8–9

Triassic period 8, 9

Triceratops 9, 23, 25, 29

Tyrannosaurus rex 9, 18, 23, 25–27, 29

Velociraptor 25

Quiz

Answer the questions to see what you have learned. Check your answers in the key below.

1. True or False: Sauropods were meat eaters.
2. What kind of dinosaurs were *Ankylosaurus* and *Stegosaurus*?
3. What was the name of the deadly dino with big crocodile-like jaws?
4. How big were *T. rex*'s eyeballs?
5. How many different species of dinosaur have scientists discovered?

1. False   2. Armored dinosaurs   3. *Spinosaurus*
4. The size of oranges   5. Over 700